CW00644581

Hai!ku

Second Edition Print 2022

First published by Hai!Hiragana 2020
www.haihiragana.com

All artwork belongs to Hai!Hiragana

ISBN 978-1-8382247-0-7

Printed & bound in UK

This book is made from
responsibly sourced paper.

Hai!ku
Japanese Kanji

Teaching the Kanji - With visuals and haiku - Making it easy

Lewis Plowman & Charlotte Martin

ルイス プラウマン ・ シャーロット マーティン

Illustrations by Martin Le Lapin

@martinlelapin • www.martinlelapin.com

Contents

Odd Radicals · 14~16
Radicals without meaning

Haiku History · 17
What is a Haiku?

Page Guide · 18~19
How to use the book

Let's Go! · 20
Time to study

The Kanji · 21~346
162 characters to learn

You Did It! · 347
You made it through

Thank You · 348~349
ありがとうございました

Bits & Bobs · 350~352
Common radicals, Kana & Index

Introduction

Hai!ku is the creation of Japan enthusiasts Lewis & Charlotte. We have been creating learning materials for Japanese ever since we started learning it ourselves. Our projects aim to take all the things we wish we knew before starting and package it up in a new, friendly and easy to understand manner.

We have been bombarded with requests for Kanji from the start, so we are very happy to release this book and we hope it will help with your studies. We are so grateful for the wonderful community of Japanese learners and would like to say thank you for all the support and kindness that has kept us going!

Challenge Accepted

So you know the Hiragana like the back of your hand and can read Katakana in your sleep. Now you want to move onto the next challenge... The infamous **Kanji!**

But where do you start? There are just so many Kanji characters (well over 45,000!) with multiple readings and meanings, it can look like an incredibly daunting task. Luckily most of these are used just for names or are very rare to see. To read a newspaper you'd need around 2,000 (which is still a lot!) It's all about breaking it down into chunks, setting clear goals and finding a method which works for you.

In this book we are covering the Kanji which very likely appear in the JLPT N5 (first level of the Japanese Language Proficiency Test). In addition, we have included basics for travel, food & signage. This covers a great range of Kanji and will introduce you to the idea of story-making so you can go on to learn even more.

Learn your Kana first!

It's a good idea to have Hiragana & Katakana under your belt before learning Kanji.
It creates the foundation for understanding the language and really does help.
In case you're rusty, check the back of the book to download kana sheets for free (p.350)

Methodology

Hai!ku aims to break down complex barriers and give you a simpler method of learning. We do that with these three ideas.

One: Start Small

Every Kanji can be broken down into simple 'puzzle pieces' called Radicals. We build up knowledge slowly and in a sequence that makes sense before introducing the more complex Kanji.

Two: Visual Learning

The radicals are turned into creative illustrations, allowing you to more easily identify them. We colour-code these and the examples which give context for how each Kanji can be used.

Three: Haiku Storytelling

Stories are a great way of making long-term memories. We use Haiku to create links between otherwise abstract radical 'puzzle pieces' to identify the whole Kanji. This way you only need to learn a handful of radicals rather than thousands of strokes.

Don't feel you have to remember the exact Haiku!
They are a starting point to inspire your own stories and links.

Finding a white whale
What are the chances of that?
One in a hundred

One thing at a time

It's debatable on whether it is best to learn the meaning and the readings at the same time or one after the other. We recommend to first focus on learning what each Kanji means and then as you learn new words the two will naturally *click* together.

Kanji Origin

The history of Kanji dates back more than 3,000 years, originating from ancient China. Kanji gets its name from the Chinese writing system called Hanzi 漢字, which means "Han character", named after the Han Dynasty.

It was brought to Japan through trade and religious missions, most likely from the closer Korean peninsula and we started to see wider use in the 5th century. Since then the phonetic Hiragana and Katakana were developed (along with Kokuji 国字, literally "national characters") which brings us to today.

3 writing systems to learn.. yay!

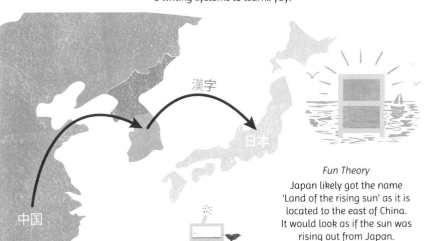

漢字

日本

中国

Fun Theory
Japan likely got the name
'Land of the rising sun' as it is
located to the east of China.
It would look as if the sun was
rising out from Japan.

日 Sun + 本 Origin = 日本 Nihon

Readings

Lifting a writing system from one language and applying it to another wasn't a straightforward task. The Chinese language uses sounds that do not exist in Japanese, so existing words needed to be worked around. A single character may be used to write one or more different words and pronounced in different ways. Kanji readings are categorized into two groups:

On'yomi	**Kun'yomi**
音読み	訓読み
The sound reading	The meaning reading
from Chinese	from native Japanese

Note that

The standalone On'yomi sound is written in Katakana as it's depicting a foreign sound.
However, it would be written with Hiragana when used in a Japanese word.
You may notice this when text is written with Furigana.
(Smaller kana reading aid shown next to Kanji text).

Radical Puzzle

Kanji originated as pictographic & ideographic drawings which made it incredibly hard to write full sentences. It would be equivalent to trying to write everything exclusively in emojis.

To simplify the writing system, scholars in the 18th century chose 214 radicals (部首 - Bushu) and used these to recreate the system. Some characters maintained their original look while others had parts substituted with the closest matching radical. Which is why some Kanji make more visual sense than others.

Radicals are basically the puzzle pieces for Kanji. Each Kanji has a 'core' radical which gives a clue to its meaning or pronunciation and how it is categorised.

For example: 男 (male) is made from 田 (rice field) + 力 (power)

*Emoji Puzzle Answer

Read - hi - ! - coo - two - learn - can - g
Read Hai!ku to learn Kanji

Some radicals are Kanji in and of themselves, such as 十 ten, 田 rice field and 木 tree. However many do not have any meaning on their own. You can think of it a little like how most letters don't mean much alone until they are used in a word.

Letters	Words	Compound Words
s a e t	East	Northeast
木 十 田	東	北東
Radicals	Kanji	Jukugo - じゅくご - 熟語

Many radicals will appear slightly different based on their position inside of a Kanji (we call these 'variations'). Sometimes squished, stretched, cut off or with altered strokes. Radicals are categorized into seven main groups according to their position.

The pink area highlights the radical's position inside the Kanji's whole (blue outer box)

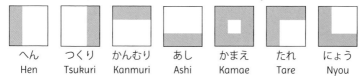

へん	つくり	かんむり	あし	かまえ	たれ	にょう
Hen	Tsukuri	Kanmuri	Ashi	Kamae	Tare	Nyou

'Common' Names

Although there isn't an official list of names for each radical, there are widely used ones. For our method, we have tweaked some of these because we found them to be confusing as they clash with an existing Kanji meaning or would be tricky to remember. Please see page 350 for a reference list.

Odd Radicals

Our method has 15 'odd radicals' which can appear inside many Kanji but don't have a reading while on their own. Some of these are the origins of Katakana which makes spotting them easier.

ト ~ Truck

Looks like a **truck** bonnet. (Katakana 'To') This also has an obscure Kanji meaning "Divination".

ル ~ Long Legs

A kangaroo bouncing along on its **long legs**. (Katakana 'Ru')

ラ ~ Ramen

Chopsticks lifting noodles from a bowl of **ramen**. (Katakana 'Ra')

ノ ~ Notebook

My **notebook** is bent. (Katakana 'No')

ム ~ Moose

One **moose** horn is larger. (Katakana 'Mu')

ナ ~ Nurse

The **nurse** is pointing the way. (Katakana 'Na')

⊥ ~ Beret

A **beret** with a thread on top.

⊓ ~ Cover

Cover the bed with a duvet.

⊓ ~ Roof

A chimney on a **roof**.

⊓ ~ Cardboard Box

Turn the **cardboard box** upside down.

∟ ~ Umbrella Handle

The top blew off my **umbrella's handle**!

⧺ ~ Leaves

A branch with five **leaves**.

| ~ Samurai Sword

Hold your **samurai sword** straight up.

聿 ~ Brushes

A selection of **brushes**.

冫 ~ Snowflakes

Two **snowflakes** sparkling.

15.

We also use 6 radicals which are Kanji but are either rare to see or a bit too advanced to learn the readings at this stage.
For now, we advise to just learn to recognise these in order to help with the Kanji they fit into.

又 ~ Again

Do you see it?
I'm seeing cute bears **again**.

寸 ~ Measure

Measure the dot with your tool.
寸 Is a unit of measurement.

尺 ~ Ruler

Looks like the letter R for **Ruler**
尺 Is a unit of distance.

斤 ~ Axe

An **axe** striking a tree.
斤 Is a unit of weight.
It's also used to count loaves of bread.

弓 ~ Bow

Pull back the string on your **bow** to fire the arrow.

士 ~ Scholar ~ Samura

A **scholar** studying about th history of the **samurai**.
(侍 is the Kanji used for Samurai, 士 indicates a socially respected job)

Haiku History

The Haiku first emerged in Japanese literature during the 17th century, though it was not known as Haiku until the 19th. Traditionally these are poems with deeper meanings, often evoking images of the natural world. Modern styles can vary widely on how closely they follow traditional elements.

They are made from three lines, totalling 17 syllables. With 5 in the first, 7 in the second and 5 again in the third.

Po|ems from Ja|pan 5
With sev|en|teen syl|lab|les 7
Like|ly are Hai|ku 5

Make your own

Our Haiku follow more of a modern style and don't usually convey deeper feelings. However, if the Kanji involves scenes of nature we have tried to keep them traditional. Just have fun! If it helps you remember the Kanji then it's done its job as a mnemonic.

Page Guide

Memory Tab
Fold over to quickly test yourself later

Visual Aid

Illustrations of the radicals used in the Kanji to help you remember the Haiku and its meaning.

Note that the radical's illustration doesn't always follow the exact Kanji shape. The idea is for you to learn to identify the puzzle pieces used by each Kanji and build upon what you have already learned.

Kanji Character

Colour-coded to highlight the radicals used inside. Follow the arrows in numerical order for the Kanji's stroke order. Using the correct order will help you memorise the Kanji and write more naturally.

Japanese comes in many font styles. Note that we use a more handwritten version of our font here.

85.

Page Front

Note that our book is arranged to be used like flashcards. We have placed the Kanji and visual aid on the front of each page with the Kanji's meaning, Haiku and readings on the back. We advise reading through the book a few times testing yourself and then turn the corner for any you find harder to remember.

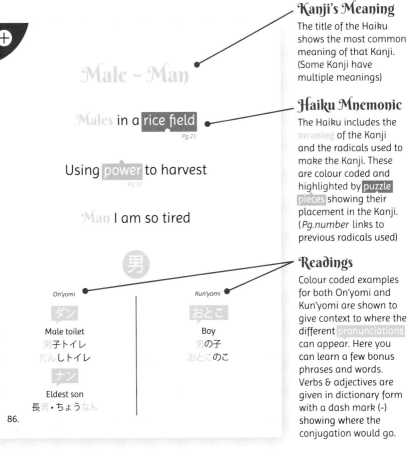

Kanji's Meaning

The title of the Haiku shows the most common meaning of that Kanji. (Some Kanji have multiple meanings)

Haiku Mnemonic

The Haiku includes the meaning of the Kanji and the radicals used to make the Kanji. These are colour coded and highlighted by puzzle pieces showing their placement in the Kanji. (Pg.number links to previous radicals used)

Readings

Colour coded examples for both On'yomi and Kun'yomi are shown to give context to where the different pronunciations can appear. Here you can learn a few bonus phrases and words. Verbs & adjectives are given in dictionary form with a dash mark (-) showing where the conjugation would go.

Male ~ Man

Males in a rice field
Pg.21

Using power to harvest
Pg.35

Man I am so tired

男

On'yomi

ダン

Male toilet
男子トイレ
だんしトイレ

ナン

Eldest son
長男・ちょうなん

Kun'yomi

おとこ

Boy
男の子
おとこのこ

86.

Let's go!
行きましょう

With all of that out of the way, you can now start learning Kanji! We recommend focusing on learning the meanings of each character first so you can identify what they mean before committing the Japanese readings to knowledge. We do hope you enjoy using our method and it helps with your studies. Good luck!

go go go

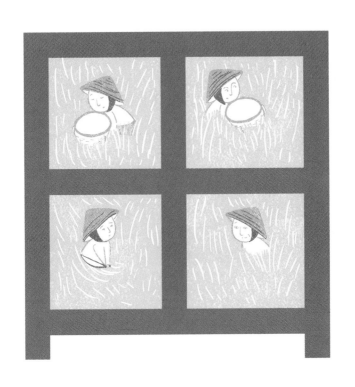

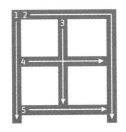

21.

Rice Field

Farmers working hard

In four adjacent **rice fields**

Collecting the crops

On'yomi	*Kun'yomi*

On'yomi

Countryside
田園
でんえん

Kun'yomi

Paddy field
田んぼ
たんぼ

Mr. Yamada (common surnam
山田さん・やまださん

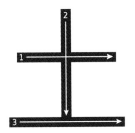

23.

Earth

From beneath the **earth**

A bean sprout is growing strong

Two leaves in the sun

On'yomi		Kun'yomi
Saturday		Garden soil
土曜日		庭の土
どようび		にわのつち

Watch Out

Visually similar to Samurai 土 but the base line is longer on **Earth** 土.

25.

Fire

Sitting by the fire

Cooking sausages on sticks

Careful not to burn

On'yomi		*Kun'yomi*
Tuesday		Fire is hot
火曜日		火は熱い
かようび		ひはあつい

Variations

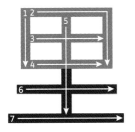

27.

Village

Outside the **village**

The people have worked the
pg.23

To create
pg.21

里

On'yomi

One hundred 'Ri'
百里
ひゃくり
(Chinese measurement
roughly 2.44 miles)

Kun'yomi

Hidden leaf village
木の葉隠れの里
このはがくれのさと

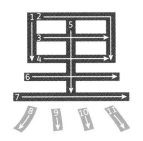

Black

 in trouble

Pg.27

We need to put out the

Pg.25 (variation)

Before it turns **black**

黒

On'yomi

コク

Blackboard
黒板
こくばん

Kun'yomi

くろ-い

Black car
黒い車
くろいくるま

White

Reading Moby Dick

It's about a fisherman

Hunting a white whale

On'yomi	Kun'yomi
ハク	しろ-い
White rice • 白米 • はくまい	White paint
ビャク	白いペンキ • しろいペンキ
Midnight sun • 白夜 • びゃくや	しら
	White snow • 白雪 • しらゆき

How interesting
The kanji spelling of おもしろい (interesting) is 面白い
Literally meaning what is in front of you is bright & clear.

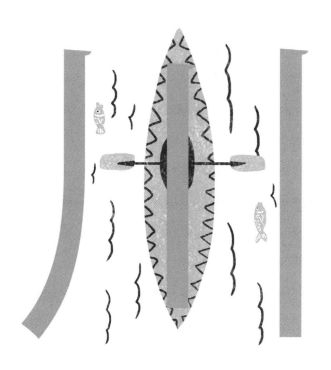

33.

River

Paddle my canoe

Do not hit the **river**bank

Stay in the middle

On'yomi

Rivers
河川
かせん

Kun'yomi

Blue river • 青い川 • あおいか

River Nile • ナイル川 • ナイルか

35.

Power ~ Strength

A black belt master

Puts his strength into a chop

Admire his power

On'yomi

リョク

Hydraulic power • 水力 • すいりょく

リキ

Sumo wrestler • 力士 • りきし

Kun'yomi

ちから

With all one's strength
力いっぱい
ちからいっぱい

Bonus Tip

Origin of Katakana 'Ka' so you can remember 'Ka' for Karate. Be careful not to confuse the readings; if you see this without other Katakana it is likely the Kanji reading.

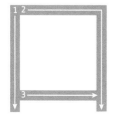

Mouth

A sleepy tiger

Mouth wide open starts to yawn

Time to go to bed

On'yomi	*Kun'yomi*
コウ	くち
Population	Lipstick • 口紅 • くちべに
人口	ぐち
じんこう	Entrance • 入口 • いりぐち

One

It's an easy one

Promise it will get more hard

There is **one** pencil

On'yomi	*Kun'yomi*
Number one (the best)	One of those
一番	その一つ
いちばん	その ひとつ
	One person
	一人
	ひとり

40.

Two

I have two pencils

But one of them is shorter

It has been used more

On'yomi	*Kun'yomi*
ニ	ふたつ
Twelve o'clock	Two doughnuts please
十二時	ドーナツを二つ下さい
じゅうにじ	ドーナツをふたつください
	ふた
	Two People
	二人
	ふたり

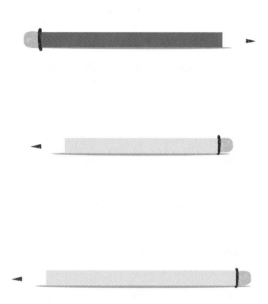

1 ──────────────▶

2

3

43.

Three

Now for simple math

You can do it in your head

Two plus one is three

pg.41　　　　*pg.39*

On'yomi

One hundred and three
百三
ひゃくさん

Kun'yomi

Three pieces
三つのかけら
みっつのかけら

44.

45.

Four

In the tiger's mouth
Pg.37

I can see some long legs
Pg.14

Eats it in *four* bites

四

On'yomi

シ

April
四月
しがつ

Kun'yomi

よん

Four hundred • 四百 • よんひゃ

よっ-つ

Four stars (rating)
四つ星 • よっつぼし

よ

Four Years • 四年 • よねん

47.

Five

Hidden in the lines

What number does it look like?

I see number *five*

On'yomi

May
五月
ごがつ

Kun'yomi

Five ice creams
五つのアイスクリーム
いつつのアイスクリーム

Fifth (of the month)
五日・いつか

49.

Seven

At my local store

The sign is upside down

Should be a **seven**

On'yomi

July
七月
しちがつ

Kun'yomi

Seven stars
七つの星
ななつのほし

Seventh (of the month)
七日・なのか

51.

Eight

Spider on a string

Does it only have two legs?

No way he has *eight*!

On'yomi	*Kun'yomi*

August・八月・はちがつ

All directions・八方・はっぽう

Eight Dorayaki
どら焼き八つ・どらやきやっ⊃

Greengrocer・八百屋・やおや

Variations

Six

Spider had eight legs
Pg.51

It got trapped by a beret
Pg.15

Now six legs are left

On'yomi

ロク

Six o'clock • 六時 • ろくじ

ロッ

Six pens • 六本のペン
ろっぽんのペン

Kun'yomi

むっつ

Six categories
六つのカテゴリー
むっつのカテゴリー

Eight inside of six

54. We put the Kanji for 6 after 8 as we arranged our method to build on radicals you've already been shown. Don't worry, counting order is the same in Japanese usually!

Nine

It's a well-known fact

That all cats have got nine lives

They are so lucky

Nine-tailed・九尾・きゅうび

September・九月・くがつ

Nine questions
九つの質問
ここのつのしつもん

Ninth (of the month)
九日・ここのか

56.

57.

Ten

Roman ten is X

Rotate it a little bit

Now it's Japanese

On'yomi

October・十月・じゅうがつ

Ten fingers・十指・じっし

Kun'yomi

10th day
十日
とおか

59.

Hundred

Finding a white whale
Pg.31

What are the chances of that?

 in a **hundred**
Pg.39

百

On'yomi	Kun'yomi
	N/A

One hundred yen coin
百円玉・ひゃくえんだま

Three hundred・三百・さんびゃく

Six hundred・六百・ろっぴゃく

61.

Thousand

Making an order

For large packs of pencils
Pg.57

Costs thousand yen
Pg.39

On'yomi

One thousand yen
千円・せんえん

Three thousand・三千・さんぜん

Kun'yomi

ち

Chiba (prefecture)
千葉・ちば

62.

Ten Thousand

What is his power?

Pg.35

It is over ten thousand

 One powerful man

Pg.39

On'yomi		Kun'yomi
 マン		*N/A*

Ten thousand yen note
一万円札
いちまんえんさつ

Small ~ Little

Little butterfly

Look at its lovely two wings

They are very small

On'yomi

Primary school
小学校
しょうがっこう

Kun'yomi

The rabbit is small
ウサギは小さい・ウサギはちいさ

Light rain・小雨・こさめ

Variations

67.

Big

Circus is in town

Clowns are wearing **big** trousers

Looks like fun to see

On'yomi

ダイ

University ・ 大学 ・ だいがく

タイ

That's tough
それは 大変ですね
それはたいへんですね

Kun'yomi

おお-きい

Large house
大きい家・おおきいいえ

お

Adult
大人・おとな

Fun Fact

You'll see these Kanji on Japanese toilets for a 大 big and 小 small flush.

69.

Heavens ~ Sky

Clown wearing big pants
Pg.67

Lifts one pencil to the sky
Pg.39

Towards the heavens

On'yomi

Weather
天気
てんき

Kun'yomi

Milky way
天の川
あまのがわ

71.

Person

Walking on two legs

This person is in no rush

Take it nice and slow

On'yomi

Foreigner・外国人・がいこくじん

10,000 people
一万人・いちまんにん

Kun'yomi

This person
この人
このひと

Variations

Tree

It is now spring time

See the blossom on the **tree**

A beautiful sight

On'yomi		*Kun'yomi*

Thursday・木曜日・もくようび

Engineering works・土木・どぼく

Sakura tree
桜の木
さくらのき

Grove

Two • **trees** • side by side

Pg.73 (x2)

Not as large as a forest

It is a small grove

On'yomi	*Kun'yomi*
Bamboo thicket	Inside the grove
竹林	林の中
ちくりん	はやしの中
	Mr. Kobayashi (common surnar
	小林さん・こばやしさん

77.

Forest ~ Woods

Three trees in the woods
Pg.73

The grove has become larger
Pg.75

Now it's a forest

On'yomi

Forest
森林
しんりん

Kun'yomi

Aomori prefecture
青森県
あおもりけん

Rest

Underneath the tree
Pg.73

The person takes a quick rest
Pg.71 (variation)

Comfy in the shade

On'yomi		Kun'yomi
キュウ		**やす-む**
Pause		Father rests
休止		父が休む・ちちがやすむ
きゅうし		**やすみ**
		Summer holiday
		夏休み・なつやすみ

80.

81.

Book ~ Origin

The wood from **one** **tree**
Pg.39 *Pg.73*

Is this paper's *origin*

Now made into *books*

本

On'yomi

Japanese (language)
日本語
にほんご

Kun'yomi

Matsumoto Castle
松本城
まつもとじょう

Counter Rule

　本 is used to count long thin objects such as pencils or chopsticks. Not books!
This is because books used to be kept on rolled-up scrolls. With the introduction of
bound books, the counter 冊 (さつ) is used and looks like pages tied by a string.
The reading alters between ホン・ボン・ポン based on the number of items counted.

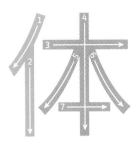

Body

In biology

Read a book on the body
Pg.81

Inside a person.
Pg.71

On'yomi	*Kun'yomi*
タイ	からだ
Body temperature	My body aches
体温	体が痛い
たいおん	からだがいたい

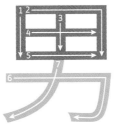

Male ~ Man

Males in a rice field
Pg.21

Using power to harvest
Pg.35

Man I am so tired

On'yomi		*Kun'yomi*
Male toilet		Boy
男子トイレ		男の子
だんしトイレ		おとこのこ
Eldest son		
長男・ちょうなん		

87.

Female ~ Woman

Dancing with a fan

Males or *females* can do it

Copy the **woman's** moves

On'yomi

Girlfriend
彼女
かのじょ

Kun'yomi

Girl (child)
女の子
おんなのこ

89.

Friend

Bear bit me again
pg.16

My *friend* took me to the nurse
pg.14

I can count on him

友

On'yomi	*Kun'yomi*
ユウ	とも
Friendship	Friend
友情	友達
ゆうじょう	ともだち

91.

Child

Child leaning over

Trying to catch their balance

While playing hopscotch

On'yomi

Microwave
電子レンジ
でんしレンジ

Kun'yomi

Child
子供
こども

93.

Mother

Flower in her hat

My *mother* is so classy

Do you not agree?

On'yomi	Kun'yomi
Home country	My mum
母国	私の母・わたしのはは
ぼこく	
	Your mother
	あなたのお母さん
	あなたのおかあさん

95.

Father

Father looks upset

I can tell he is frowning

Hope he is okay

On'yomi

Grandfather
祖父
そふ

Kun'yomi

My dad
私の父・わたしのちち

Your father
あなたのお父さん
あなたのおとうさん

96.

Like

Woman and her child
pg.87 pg.91

Playing hopscotch in the park

They like these moments

On'yomi	Kun'yomi
On'yomi	*Kun'yomi*

コウ

Curiosity
好奇心
こうきしん

す-き

I like ramen
ラーメンが好きです
ラーメンがすきです

99.

School

While playing at school

Lost my beret up a tree
Pg.15 · Pg.73

My dad got it down
Pg.95

Kanji: 校

On'yomi

コウ

School
学校
がっこう

Kun'yomi

N/A

101.

Letter

I have taught my child
Pg.91

Helicopters land on roofs
Pg.15

On the letter 'H'

On'yomi

ジ

Kanji
漢字
かんじ

Kun'yomi

N/A

Learning ~ Study

A child covering
Pg.91 *Pg.15*

Homework with small study notes
Pg.65 (variation)

While he is learning

On'yomi	Kun'yomi
ガク	まな-ぶ
Student	Learn Japanese
学生・がくせい	日本語を学ぶ
ガッ-	にほんごをまなぶ
School	
学校・がっこう	

105.

Eye

With my monocle

My **eye** looks super stylish

Like a gentleman

On'yomi	Kun'yomi
On'yomi	*Kun'yomi*

Subject (course at school)
科目
かもく

Green eyes
緑色の目
みどりいろのめ

107.

Ear

While at the barbers

Wearing headphones in his **ears**

Listening to tunes

On'yomi	Kun'yomi
On'yomi	*Kun'yomi*

ENT doctor
耳鼻咽喉科
じびいんこうか

Long ears
長い耳
ながいみみ

Hand

A sign of respect

Do a fist bump with your hand

When you say 'hello'

On'yomi

Clapping (applause)
拍手
はくしゅ

Kun'yomi

Letter (post)
手紙
てがみ

Variations

Foot ~ Leg

Stand in a foot bath

Pull your trousers up your leg

So they don't get wet

On'yomi	Kun'yomi
A pair of socks 一足の靴下 いっそくのくつした	Footsteps (sound of) 足音・あし おと
	Add three to two to get five 三に二を足すと五になる さんににをたすとごになる

113.

Nail ~ Claw ~ Talon

The nails of a bird

What do you call them again?

Their claws or talons

On'yomi

Clutches (devious plan)
爪牙
そうが

Kun'yomi

Nail clippers・爪切り・つめきり

Toothpick
爪楊枝・つまようじ

Variations

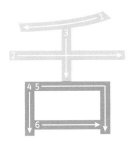

Tongue

Inside of your mouth
Pg.37

You have thousands of taste buds
Pg.61

All over your *tongue*

On'yomi	*Kun'yomi*
Articulation	Long tongue
滑舌	長い舌
かつぜつ	ながいした

Say

Poet is speaking

Has a lot of words to say

In a melody

On'yomi	Kun'yomi
Language	He says
言語・げんご	彼は言う・かれはいう
Message (verbal)	Word
伝言・でんごん	言葉・ことば

118.

119.

Language ~ Word

 give a speech
Pg.47   Pg.37

What language are the words in?

I  Japanese
Pg.117

On'yomi

Japanese language
日本語
にほん ご

Kun'yomi

Let a secret slip
語るに落ちる
かたるにおちる

Talk

Start with a deep breath

Use your tongue to say the words

Pg.115 *Pg.117*

To **talk** in public

On'yomi	Kun'yomi

On'yomi

ワ

Phone call
電話
でんわ

Kun'yomi

はな-す
When speaking
話すとき・はなすとき

はなし
Discussion
話し合い・はなしあい

123.

Gold

In northern Kyoto

There's a temple painted gold

It's well worth a trip

On'yomi

Friday
金曜日
きんようび

Kun'yomi

Money
お金
おかね

125.

Moon ~ Month

Landing on the moon

Took a whole month to get there

It was a long trip

On'yomi	*Kun'yomi*
Monday	Bright moon
月曜日・げつようび	明るい月
	あかるいつき
April	
四月・しがつ	

127.

Sun ~ Day ~ Japan

The sun is rising

Over the coast of Japan

It is a new day

On'yomi	Kun'yomi
Sunday • 日曜日 • にちようび	Sunrise • 日の出 • ひので
Japan • 日本 • にほん	Sunday • 日曜日 • にちようび
Another day • 後日 • ごじつ	Fourth (of the month) • 四日 • よっ

128.

129.

Bright ~ Light

The full moon is bright
Pg.125

Reflecting light from the sun
Pg.127

Up in the night sky

On'yomi	Kun'yomi
On'yomi	*Kun'yomi*
メイ	あか-るい
Proof	Bright person (cheerful)
証明	明るい人
しょうめい	あかるいひと
	あ
	Tomorrow night
	明日の夜・あしたのよる

131.

Stand Up ~ Rise

Doing lots of squats

My legs aching when I **rise**

It's hard to **stand up**

On'yomi

National
国立
こくりつ

Kun'yomi

Stand on the bus
バスで立つ
バスでたつ

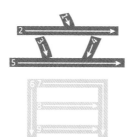

133.

Sound ~ Noise

Would you hear a **sound**

Standing on the sun's surface
Pg.131   *Pg.127*

Or no **noise** at all

On'yomi	*Kun'yomi*
Music	Sound of the wind
音楽	風音・かざおと
おんがく	
	Timbre (musical sound)
	音色・ねいろ

Dark ~ Shadow

As the sun goes down
Pg.127

Strange •noises• come from **shadows**
Pg.133

Hidden in the **dark**

On'yomi	*Kun'yomi*
PIN (personal identification number)	It is dark outside
暗証番号	外は暗いです
あんしょうばんごう	そとはくらいです

137.

Evening

Missed the last train home

It is late in the **evening**

Hailing a taxi

On'yomi

Short period of time
一朝一夕
いっちょういっせき

Kun'yomi

Evening meal
夕飯
ゆうはん

Bonus Tip
Looks like Katakana タ 'Ta' so you can remember that in
the **evening** you take a タクシー 'taxi' home.

139.

Many ~ Frequent

During the
Pg.137 (x2)

I **frequently** see taxis

There are too **many**

多

On'yomi	Kun'yomi
タ	おお-い
Probably	Tokyo has a large population
多分	東京は人口が多いです
たぶん	とうきょうはじんこうがおおいて

タクシー!

141.

Name ~ Famous

Saw someone *famous*

Shouted their name with my mouth
Pg.37

The other evening
Pg.137

名

On'yomi

 メイ

Celebrity
有名人・ゆうめいじん

 ミョウ

Surname
名字・みょうじ

Kun'yomi

 な

Given name
名前
なまえ

143.

Oneself

Point towards your nose

When you indicate oneself

When you're in Japan

On'yomi

ジ

Bike・自転車・じてんしゃ

シ

Nature・自然・しぜん

Kun'yomi

みずか-ら

By choice (free will)
自ら進んで・みずからすすん゛

おの-ず

Naturally・自ずと・おのずと

Fun Fact

In western countries, you'd typically point to your chest to indicate yourself
whereas in Japan you'd point at your nose.

外

145.

Outside

The other evening.
Pg.137

I heard a loud noise outside

Truck hit a taxi
Pg.14

外

On'yomi	Kun'yomi
ガイ	そと
Foreign country	Exterior
外国・がいこく	外側
ゲ	そとがわ
Surgery	
外科・げか	

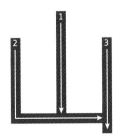

147.

Mountain

Three peaks rising up

Snow on top of the **mountain**

Cold air whistles by

On'yomi

Mt. Fuji・富士山・ふじさん

Volcano・火山・かざん

Kun'yomi

Over the mountain
山の上
やまのうえ

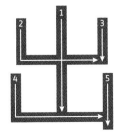

149.

Go Out ~ Put Out ~ Exit

Go out of your tent

When you *exit* the **mountains**

Pg.147 (x2)

Put out the campfire

On'yomi	*Kun'yomi*
Going out • 外出 • がいしゅつ	To answer the phone 電話に出る • でんわにでる
Publication • 出版 • しゅっぱん	Take out money お金を出す • おかねをだす

151.

Enter

Camping in the wild

The wind echoes through the trees

I **enter** my tent

On'yomi	*Kun'yomi*
ニュウ	い -れる
Enrolment (at school) 入学 にゅうがく	To insert a card in the ATM カードをATMに入れる カードをATMにいれる
	はい -る
	To enter university 大学に入る・だいがくにはいる

153.

Dry

The sun is shining

Hang my washing up to dry

Blowing in the wind

On'yomi

Drought (dry weather)
干魃

かんばつ

Kun'yomi

Dry outside (in the sun)
外で干す
そとでほす

155.

Tall ~ High ~ Expensive

A **tall** skyscraper

How much does a **high** room cost?

Very **expensive**

On'yomi	Kun'yomi
On'yomi	*Kun'yomi*
コウ	たか-い
High quality	It's expensive eh?
高品質	高いですね
こうひんしつ	たかいですね

157.

Cheap ~ Peaceful ~ Safe

Safe under her roof
Pg.15

The woman feels so peaceful
Pg.87

Staying in is cheap

158.

159.

Knife ~ Sword

You must be careful

Using a Japanese knife

It's sharp as a sword

On'yomi

Sword smith
刀工
とうこう

Kun'yomi

Samurai sword
武士の刀・ぶしのかたな

Razor・剃刀・かみそり

Variations

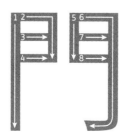

Gate

Ride to the castle

But the guard won't let me in

The **gate** has been closed

On'yomi

Park gate
公園の門
こうえんのもん

Kun'yomi

A traditional pine decoration
門松
かどまつ

Interval ~ Between

Guards **between** the gates

Pg.161

Standing for long *intervals*

Throughout the whole

Pg.127

On'yomi

One year (period of time)
一年間
いちねん かん

Kun'yomi

あいだ

Between us
私たちの間・わたしたちのあい

Living room・居間・いま

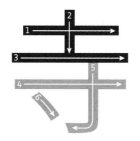

165.

Temple

 the statue
Pg.16

Outside the Buddhist temple

Built upon the earth
Pg.23

On'yomi

Temple (place of worship)
寺院
じいん

Kun'yomi

Go to the temple
お寺に行く
おてらにいく

167.

Time ~ Hour

Planning out the day
Pg.127

Visiting Buddhist • temples
Pg.165

Left time for five hours

On'yomi		Kun'yomi
ジ		とき
Four o'clock		Sometimes
四時		時々
よじ		ときどき

Bonus Haiku

Measure on the earth ~ A shadow cast by the sun ~ You can tell the time.

Minute ~ Part

Chopping with a knife
Pg.159

In a matter of minutes

Cut into eight parts
Pg.51

On'yomi

Probably・多分・たぶん

Every minute・毎分・まいふん

One tenth・一分・いちぶ

Kun'yomi

I understand this
私はこれが分かる
わたしはこれがわかる

Divide into three
三つに分ける・みっつにわけ

170.

Noon

My notebook got wet
Pg.14

Hang it up until its dry
Pg.153

In the **noon** sun's heat

On'yomi		*Kun'yomi*
		N/A
Afternoon (p.m.)		
午後		
ごご		

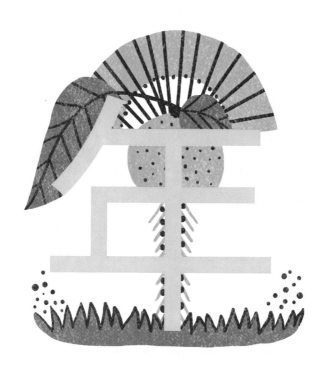

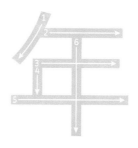

Year

New year in Japan

Two mochi and an orange

Are put on display

On'yomi

ネン

Last year
昨年
さくねん

Kun'yomi

とし

This year
今年
ことし

Kagami Mochi (鏡餅 "Mirror Rice Cake")
A traditional Japanese decoration said to bring good luck in the new year.

174.

Now

Person walking by
Pg.71

A ramen stall that smells good
Pg.14

Now they want a bite

On'yomi	Kun'yomi
Good evening	Now it's five o'clock
今晩は	今は五時です
こんばんは	いまはごじです

177.

Early ~ Fast

Sunday ten a.m.
Pg.127 *Pg.57*

I was meant to wake *early*

Now I must move *fast*

On'yomi	Kun'yomi

Early morning
早朝・そうちょう

Immediately
早速・さっそく

You've got time (still early)
まだ早いよ
まだはやいよ

179.

Water

Caring for my plant

Two droplets fall from the leaf

As I water it

On'yomi

スイ

Wednesday
水曜日
すいようび

Kun'yomi

みず

Water please
お水をください
お みずをください

Variations

Every

In  mother's notebook
Pg.93   *Pg.14*

I am given one gold star
Pg.39

Every time I'm good

毎

On'yomi

マイ

Every day
毎日
まいにち

Kun'yomi

ごと

Monthly
月毎
つきごと

183.

Ocean

Follow the water
Pg.179

Every river leads to here
Pg.181

Towards the ocean

On'yomi

Ocean
海洋
かいよう

Kun'yomi

Blue sea
青い海
あおいうみ

185.

Half

Left my clothes to
Pg.153

But it rained a little bit
Pg.65 (variation)

They are still half wet

半

On'yomi

Half past three
三時半
さんじはん

Kun'yomi

Middle of the month
月半ば
つきなかば

Bonus Tip

Imagine three sticks in a row with the top stick being broken in half by a samurai sword.

187.

Hear ~ Ask ~ Listen

To hear what you ask

Place your ear against the gate
Pg.107 *Pg.161*

Then listen closely

Pg.107 *Pg.161*

On'yomi

Newspaper
新聞
しんぶん

Kun'yomi

Hear a noise
物音を聞く・ものおとをきく

A dog can be heard
犬の鳴き声が聞こえる
いぬのなきごえがきこえる

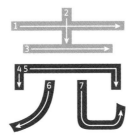

189.

Sell

Sell large bed covers
Pg.15

To the scholar with long legs
Pg.16   *Pg.14*

Keep him warm at night

On'yomi

Buying and selling
売買
ばいばい

Kun'yomi

Sell this
これを売る
これをうる

191.

Read

When you a book
Pg.189

You have to what's inside
Pg.117

So they want to read

On'yomi		*Kun'yomi*
ドク		よ-む
Reading		Read a book
読書		本を読む
どくしょ		ほんをよむ

Write

Practice every day
Pg.127

With bottled ink and brushes
Pg.15

You can **write** Kanji

On'yomi		*Kun'yomi*
Dictionary		Write Hiragana
辞書		ひらがなを書く
じしょ		ひらがなをかく

Eat ~ Food

Look inside the fridge

For something that you can *eat*

Look at all the *food*

On'yomi

Meal
食事
しょくじ

Kun'yomi

I love eating!
私は食べるのが大好きです
わたしはたべるのがだいすきて

197.

Look ~ See

In my opinion

Your eyes can look and see more
Pg.105

If you have long legs
Pg.14

見

On'yomi	*Kun'yomi*
ケン	み-る
Opinion	Watch a bird・鳥を見る・とりをみ
意見	み-せる
いけん	Show the shoes
	靴を見せる・くつをみせる
	み
	Blossom viewing・花見・はな

198.

199.

Go ~ Act ~ Line

Go to the island

Line up with your telescope

Act and turn the ship

On'yomi	Kun'yomi
Bank	Walk to school
銀行・ぎんこう	歩いて学校に行く
	あるいてがっこうにいく
Queue	Hold a match・試合を行う
行列・ぎょうれつ	しあいをおこなう

Meeting

During their *meeting*

Two people discuss the price

Pg.41 *Pg.71*

Trading for a **moose**

Pg.14

On'yomi

カイ

Company
会社
かいしゃ

Kun'yomi

あ-う

Meet friends
友達に会う
ともだちにあう

202.

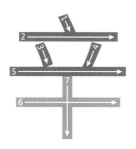

203.

Spicy ~ Hot

Eat spicy wings
Pg.57

 up and shout from the pain
Pg.131

They are way too

辛

On'yomi

シン

Patience
辛抱
しんぼう

Kun'yomi

から-い

Spicy flavour
辛い味
からいあじ

205.

Spirit ~ Air ~ Mood

There is a good **mood**

You can feel it in the **air**

Our **spirits** are high

On'yomi | *Kun'yomi*

Healthy
元気・げんき

Sleepiness
眠気・ねむけ

N/A

206.

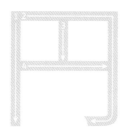

Yen ~ Circle ~ Round

Yen coins must be round

To use this vending machine

A perfect circle

On'yomi	Kun'yomi
One yen	This coin is round
一円	このコインは円い
いち<ruby>えん</ruby>	このコインは<ruby>まるい</ruby>

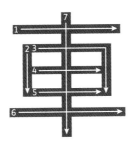

Car ~ Vehicle

See my brand new **car**

A four-seater **vehicle**

So much fun to drive

On'yomi

Automobile
自動車
じどうしゃ

Kun'yomi

Go by car
車で行きます
くるまでいきます

Bonus Haiku
Count the **vehicles** ~ ten **cars** above and below ~ driving by a field

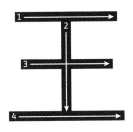

211.

King

Sitting in a throne

The **king** is holding his sword

He rules the country

On'yomi		*Kun'yomi*
オウ		*N/A*
King		
国王		
こくおう		

213.

Emperor

Roman emperor

He was like the king of Rome
Pg.211

Dressed in red and white
Pg.31

On'yomi

Imperial Palace
皇居
こうきょ

Kun'yomi

N/A

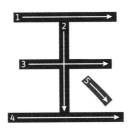

215.

Ball ~ Jewel

On the old king's cheek
Pg.211

A ball of snowflakes sparkles
Pg.15 (one shard)

Shines like a jewel

Throne
玉座
ぎょくざ

Kun'yomi

Onion
玉ねぎ・たまねぎ

Eyeball
目玉・めだま

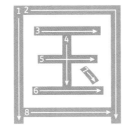

Country

Fans shout with their mouths
Pg.37

For their **country's** foot ball team
Pg.215

To show their support

国

On'yomi

コク

Foreign language
外国語
がいこくご

Kun'yomi

くに

What country did you come fro[m]
どこの国から来ましたか
どこのくにからきましたか

219.

Capital

Heard by word of mouth
Pg.37

A small beret is trendy
Pg.65   *Pg.15*

In the capital

On'yomi

Kyoto
京都・きょうと

Beijing
北京・ぺきん

Kun'yomi

N/A

221.

Park ~ Garden

Inside the stone wall

Hidden **park** with a fountain

Gardens and a pond

On'yomi		Kun'yomi
On'yomi		*Kun'yomi*

エン

Zoo
動物園
どうぶつえん

その

Bamboo garden
竹の園
たけのその

Bonus Haiku

The capital's **park** ~ Has ten beautiful gardens ~ I am open-mouthed.

222.

All ~ Whole

In the **whole** country

Each person will pay their tax

Pg.71

All goes to the

Pg.211

全

On'yomi

Altogether
全部
ぜんぶ

Kun'yomi

Entirely different
全く違う
まったくちがう

225.

Public ~ Official

In the **public** park

Eight large moose are on the loose

Pg.51 (variation)   *Pg.14*

It is **official**

公

On'yomi

コウ

Public park
公園
こうえん

Kun'yomi

おおやけ

Make public
公にする
おおやけにする

227.

Private ~ Me ~ I

I hide in a tree
Pg.73

Looking for somewhere private

One moose can see me
Pg.39　　　*Pg.14*

私

On'yomi

シ

Private use
私用
しよう

Kun'yomi

わたし

I am Lewis
私はルイスです
わたしはルイスです

228.

229.

Craft ~ Construction

In the **construction**

Of the elevator door

Is good **craft**smanship

Factory
工場・こうじょう

Scheme
工夫・くふう

Left

Nurse turned to the **left**
Pg.14

Past the new **construction** site
Pg.229

When she left from work

On'yomi

Left-wing (politics)
左翼
さよく

Kun'yomi

Left hand
左手
ひだりて

233.

Right

The **nurse** said turn right
Pg.14

Heard it come out of her **mouth**
Pg.37

She is always right

On'yomi

Turning to the right
右折・うせつ

Left and right
左右・さゆう

Kun'yomi

Right hand-side
右側
みぎがわ

235.

East

Ten **rice fields** growing
Pg.57 *Pg.21*

Trees pink with cherry blossom
Pg.73

Find them in the east

On'yomi		*Kun'yomi*
Tokyo		East Japan
東京		東日本
とうきょう		ひがしにほん

237.

West ~ Spain

A surfer from **Spain**

Catches waves on the **west** coast

While on holiday

On'yomi	Kun'yomi
On'yomi	*Kun'yomi*

The west • 西洋 • せいよう

Kansai • 関西 • かんさい

Watermelon • 西瓜 • すいか

Western Japan
西日本
にしにほん

238.

South

In a **cardboard box**

Pg.15

Are **ten** pieces of chicken

Pg.57

Southern **hot** flavour

Pg.203

On'yomi

ナン

South East
東南
とうなん

Kun'yomi

みなみ

South exit
南口
みなみぐち

240.

241.

North

In their sleeping bags

A father and son gaze up

The North star shines bright

On'yomi

North East
東北・とうほく

Hokkaido
北海道・ほっかいどう

Kun'yomi

North Wind
北風
きたかぜ

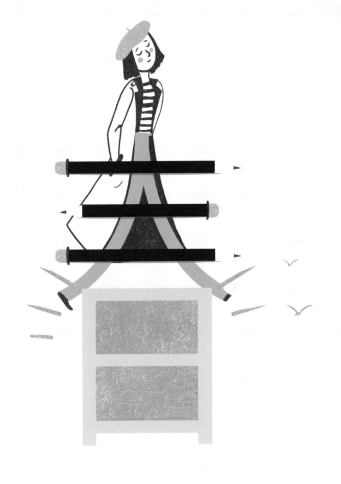

Spring

 feels the sun

Pg.71   Pg.127

Three months into the new year

Pg.43

It is the spring time

On'yomi		Kun'yomi
Spring (season)		Spring vacation
春季		春休み
しゅんき		はるやすみ

245.

Winter

In the **winter** time

Grab two skis and head outside

To enjoy the snow

On'yomi

Winter (season)
冬季
とうき

Kun'yomi

Winter holiday
冬休み
ふゆやすみ

247.

Summer

During the winter

Pg.245 (variation)

One finds oneself longing for

Pg.39 *Pg.143*

The heat of summer

On'yomi	Kun'yomi
カ	なつ
Summer (season)	Summer time
夏季・かき	夏場
	なつば
ゲ	
Summer solstice	
夏至・ゲシ	

Autumn

Trees with fire colour
Pg.73　　　*Pg.25*

One leaf swaying in the wind
Pg.39

It is autumn time

On'yomi		Kun'yomi
Autumn (season)		Beginning of autumn
秋季		秋口
しゅうき		あきぐち

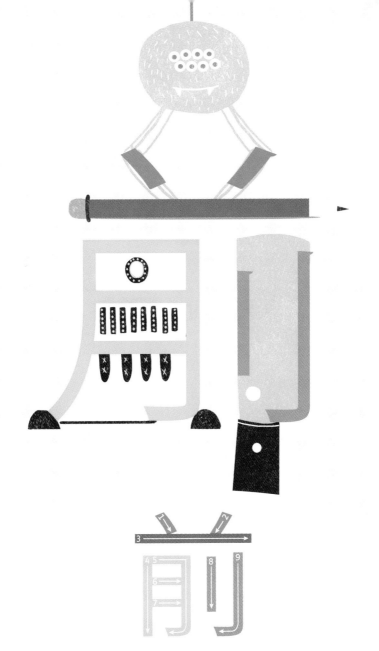

251.

Before ~ In front

In front of the moon

Pg.125

Before the sword made a sound
Pg.159 (variation)

Cut one into eight

Pg.39   *Pg.51 (variation)*

前

On'yomi

ゼン

Morning (a.m.)
午前

ごぜん

Kun'yomi

まえ

Three years ago
三年前
さんねんまえ

252.

253.

Behind ~ Back ~ Later

In a winter storm
Pg.245 (variation)

My two moose got left behind
Pg.14 (doubled)

I'll go back later
Pg.199 (left part)

On'yomi	*Kun'yomi*
ゴ	**のち**
Another day	Later・後ほど・のちほど
後日・ごじつ	
コウ	**あと**
	Postponing・後回し・あとまわ
Latter half	**うし-ろ**
後半・こうはん	Behind the car
	車の後ろ・くるまのうしろ

255.

Above ~ Up

High **above** the ground

She balances carefully

Everyone looks **up**

On'yomi	*Kun'yomi*

On'yomi

ジョウ

Good at (skilful)
上手
じょうず

Kun'yomi

うえ

Above me・私の上・わたしのう

あが-る

To stand up・立ち上がる・たちあた

のぼる

Ascend the stairs
階段を上る・かいだんをのぼ

257.

Below ~ Down

On the climbing wall

Below me is a great drop

Scary to look **down**

On'yomi

Descending a mountain
下山・げざん

Underground (Metro)
地下鉄・ちかてつ

Kun'yomi

Socks・靴下・くつした

Lower a rope
ロープを下げる・ロープをさ…

Go downhill・坂を下る・さかをく…

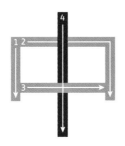

259.

Middle ~ In

A sword swallower

In the middle of his mouth
Pg.37

A samurai sword
Pg.15

On'yomi		*Kun'yomi*
China		Midnight
中国・ちゅうごく		夜中
		よなか
All day long		
一日中・いちにちじゅう		

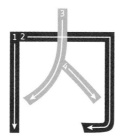

261.

Inside

The person shouts loud
Pg.71

What's **inside** the cardboard box?
Pg.15

It's a mystery

On'yomi

Domestic
国内
こくない

Kun'yomi

Shyness
内気
うちき

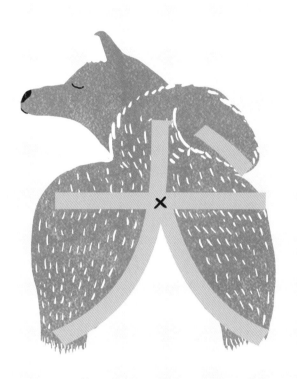

263.

Dog

I love Shiba dogs

Especially when they walk

Shaking their bottoms

On'yomi	Kun'yomi
On'yomi	*Kun'yomi*

Watchdog
番犬
ばんけん

Puppy
子犬
こいぬ

Shellfish

Open eight shellfish
Pg.51

My eye see something sparkle
Pg.105

A beautiful pearl

On'yomi	Kun'yomi
On'yomi	*Kun'yomi*
バイ	かい
Shell money	I can't eat shellfish
貝貨	貝が食べられません
ばいか	かいがたべられません

267.

Horse

Wearing a bridle

The **horse** is ready to race

On its four quick legs

On'yomi

Foolish
馬鹿らしい
ばからしい

Kun'yomi

Stable
馬小屋
うまごや

269.

Fish

Making sashimi

Cutting fresh *fish* on a board

He's made four so far

On'yomi

Goldfish
金魚
きんぎょ

Kun'yomi

Fishing
魚釣り・さかなつり

Fish market
魚市場・うおいちば

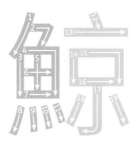

271.

Whale

The size of a **whale**

Is huge like a capital

Pg.219

Compared to a fish

Pg.269

鯨

On'yomi	*Kun'yomi*
ゲイ	くじら
White whale	Whale song
白鯨	鯨の唄
はくげい	くじらのうた

273.

Cow

Standing in a field

There is a **cow** with two horns

Mooing happily

On'yomi

Beef
牛肉
ぎゅうにく

Kun'yomi

Calf
小牛
こうし

Sheep

Two horns on its head

Horizontal eye pupils

Has to be a **sheep**

On'yomi

Wool
羊毛
ヨウモウ

Kun'yomi

Lamb
子羊
こひつじ

277.

Bird ~ Chicken

Inside the bird nest

Little chicken looking up

Calling to be fed

On'yomi

Swan
白鳥
はくちょう

Kun'yomi

Torii gate
鳥居
とりい
(Shrine archway)

279.

Meat

Inside the sandwich
Pg.261

The person adds in lettuce
Pg.71

With slices of **meat**

On'yomi

Pork
豚肉
ぶたにく

Kun'yomi

N/A

Vegetable

Use your to dig
Pg.113

Through the **leaves** under the **tree**
Pg.15   *Pg.73*

Find *vegetables*

菜

<table>
<tr><td>On'yomi</td><td></td><td>Kun'yomi</td></tr>
<tr><td>サイ</td><td></td><td>な</td></tr>
<tr><td>Vegetables</td><td></td><td>Leaf vegetables</td></tr>
<tr><td>野菜</td><td></td><td>菜っ葉</td></tr>
<tr><td>やさい</td><td></td><td>なっぱ</td></tr>
</table>

283.

Rice ~ USA

Twenty types of rice

Are grown in the USA

Sprouting from the ground

On'yomi

Polished rice (white rice)
白米・はくまい

North America
北米・ほくべい

Kun'yomi

Grain of rice
米粒
こめつぶ

Fruit

In a field  of trees

Pg.21   *Pg.73*

The farmer tends to his fruit

To achieve ripeness

On'yomi	Kun'yomi
カ	**は-たす**
Fruits (of one's labour)	Accomplish a mission
成果	使命を果たす
せいか	しめいをはたす
	くだ
	Fruit
	果物・くだもの

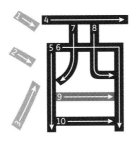

287.

Sake ~ Alcohol

Sake from the **west**
Pg.237

With **one** percent alcohol
Pg.39

Tastes just like **water**
Pg.179

On'yomi	*Kun'yomi*
Refined sake	Drink sake
清酒	酒を飲む・さけをのむ
せいしゅ	
	Alcohol shop
	酒店・さかだな

289.

Tea

To make matcha **tea**

A person covers the tree
Pg.71 *Pg.73 (edited)*

Gives the flavour
Pg.15

茶

On'yomi	*Kun'yomi*
チャ	*N/A*
Matcha 抹茶・まっちゃ	
サ	
The way of tea (ceremony) 茶道・さどう	

Milk

Child's · nails tear the box
Pg.91 · *Pg.113*

Hold your · umbrella handle
Pg.15

Now it's raining milk

On'yomi	*Kun'yomi*
Cow milk	Milk is white
牛乳	乳は白い・ちちはしろい
ぎゅうにゅう	
	Udder
	乳房・ちぶさ

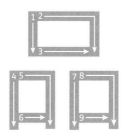

293.

Goods

Three ingredients

Cooked and prepared into *goods*

Ready for your mouths

Pg.37(x3)

On'yomi

ヒン

Food products
食品
しょくひん

Kun'yomi

しな

Out of stock
品切れ
しなぎれ

Bonus Tip
Looks like three boxes of goods stacked up.

294.

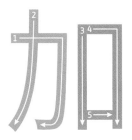

Add ~ Join

It takes a strong·mouth
Pg.35   Pg.37

To **add** lots of chilli sauce

Join me in the pain

On'yomi

カ

Jamaica
牙買加
ジャマイカ

Kun'yomi

Add milk
牛乳を加える
ぎゅうにゅうをくわえる

O Canada

加 is also the Kanji used to represent Canada.

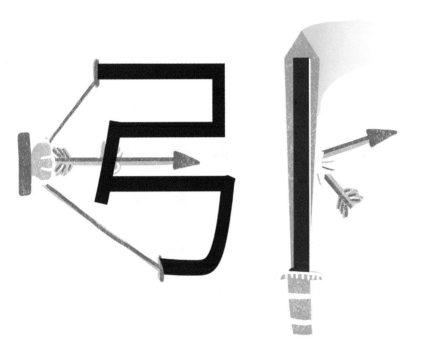

Pull

Pull back your <mark>bow</mark> string
Pg.16

<mark>Samurai sword</mark> strikes the shot
Pg.15

Cuts the arrow down

On'yomi

Quotation
引用
いんよう

Kun'yomi

Draw a line
線を引く
せんをひく

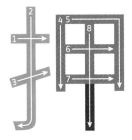

Push

Fight in the rice field
Pg.21

Samurai swords in both hands
Pg.15   *Pg.109 (variation)*

Push back the enemy

On'yomi	*Kun'yomi*
オウ	お-す
Confiscation	Push a bicycle
押収	自転車を押す
おうしゅう	じてんしゃをおす

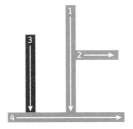

301.

Stop

Up • above the ground
Pg.255

Samurai sword • cuts the rope
Pg.15

She suddenly stops

On'yomi	Kun'yomi
シ	
Ban (prohibition)	Stop sleeping
禁止	寝るのを止める・ねるのをやめ
きんし	
	Stop the car
	車を止める・くるまをとめる

Come

Ate 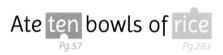 ten bowls of rice
Pg.57   *Pg.283*

I want to eat even more

The next time I **come**

来

On'yomi

 ライ

Next month
来月
らいげつ

Kun'yomi

 く-る

Coming year・来る年・くるとし

こ-ない

Don't come please
来ないでください・こないでくださ

 き-ます

Are you coming?・来ますか・きます

305.

Before ~ Previous

Before today's cows

Pg.273 (base removed)

Previous generations

Used to have long legs

Pg.14

先

On'yomi	*Kun'yomi*
セン	さき
Teacher	Five miles ahead
先生	五マイル先
せんせい	ごマイルさき

307.

Life ~ Birth

From **birth** throughout **life**

How much gas can a  make?

Pg.273

 hundred kilos

Pg.39

生

On'yomi	*Kun'yomi*
セイ	い-きる
Life・生活・せいかつ	Live happily
ショウ	幸せに生きる・しあわせにいき
Ginger・生姜・しょうが	なま
-ジョウ	Draft beer・生ビール・なまビー
Birthday・誕生日・たんじょうび	うまれる
308.	Born from・から生まれる
	からうまれる

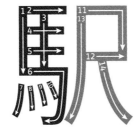

Station

Horses • were the best
Pg.267

But now that we have stations

Use a J•R train
Pg.16

On'yomi		Kun'yomi
		N/A
Next station		
次の駅		
つぎのえき		

JR Trains

JR stands for Japan Railways. The JR pass is a must-have for tourists wanting to explore!

310.

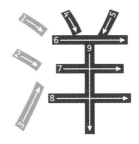

311.

Western style ~ Ocean

Food boiled in water.
Pg.179 (variation)

From far across the ocean

Western style sheep stew
Pg.275

On'yomi	Kun'yomi
ヨウ	*N/A*
Western cuisine (Japan style) 洋食 ようしょく	

313.

Show ~ Display

Win a big trophy

Put it in a *display* case

Show it off with pride

Exhibition
展示・てんじ

To imply
示唆する・しさする

Kun'yomi

Show an example
例を示す
れいをしめす

314.

315.

Forbid ~ Ban

Hidden in the grove
Pg.75

Seeing the display is **ban**ned
Pg.313

I must **forbid** it

On'yomi		Kun'yomi
		N/A
No smoking		
禁煙		
きんえん		

317.

Transform ~ Change

Over seven days
Pg.49 (edited)

A person changes to fox
Pg.71 (variation)

Transforms in a week

On'yomi	Kun'yomi
カ	ば-ける
Chemistry	A fox takes the shape of a hum
化学・かがく	キツネが人間に化ける
 ケ	キツネがにんげんにばける
Makeup	
化粧・けしょう	

318.

319.

Flower

Winter turns to spring

The dark green leaves are transformed
Pg.15 *Pg.317*

Bursting with flowers

On'yomi	*Kun'yomi*
Vase (for flowers)	Firework
花瓶	花火
びん	

321.

Nothing ~ None

Shadows of jail bars

None are able to escape

Nothing can get out

On'yomi

Free (no charge)
無料・むりょう

Safety
無事・ぶじ

Kun'yomi

Idiom like 'the grass is greener'
無いものねだり
ないものねだり

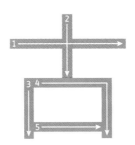

323.

old

Ten years out of date
Pg.57

Don't put that sweet in your mouth
Pg.37

Because it is old

On'yomi	*Kun'yomi*
Second-hand (used)	This phone is old
中古	その電話は古いです
ちゅうこ	そのでんわはふるいです

325.

New

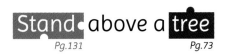

Stand • above a tree
Pg.131   *Pg.73*

Testing out my brand new • axe
Pg.16

Test how sharp it is

On'yomi	*Kun'yomi*

Shinkansen (bullet train)	New book
新幹線	新しい本 • あたらしい ほん
しん かんせん	
	New (discovery)
	新たな発見 • あらた なはっけん

326.

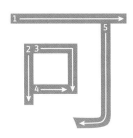

Passable ~ Can

Checking a small gem

Passable as a diamond

Can it be a fake?

On'yomi		*Kun'yomi*
		N/A
Cute		
可愛い		
かわいい		

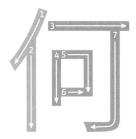

329.

What?

What's the person's goal?
Pg.71

Have passable Japanese
Pg.327

For their Japan trip

On'yomi	Kun'yomi
Geometry	What is this?
幾何学	それは何ですか・それはなんです
きかがく	
	What will you eat?
	何を食べますか・なにをたべます

331.

Trees **white** with **snow flakes**

Pg.73 Pg.31 Pg.15

The wind jingles like music

It gives me comfort

On'yomi	*Kun'yomi*

Music	Karaoke is enjoyable
音楽・おんがく	カラオケは楽しい
	カラオケはたのしい
Paradise	

333.

Medicine ~ Chemical

Chemicals from leaves
Pg.15

A natural medicine

Used to bring comfort
Pg.331

On'yomi

Medicine (products)
薬品・やくひん

Pharmacy
薬局・やっきょく

Kun'yomi

Drugstore
薬屋
くすりや

335.

Lake

Very  old water
Pg.323　　　*Pg.179*

Underneath the moon's surface
Pg.125

In an ancient *lake*

 湖

On'yomi

コ

Lake shore
湖畔
こはん

Kun'yomi

 みずうみ

Swan lake
白鳥の湖
はくちょうのみずうみ

337.

Cave ~ Hole

Look at the **cave** roof
Pg.15

Something glistens from a **hole**

Eight eyes looking back
Pg.51

On'yomi	Kun'yomi
ケツ	あな
Dig one's own grave	The sweater has a hole
墓穴を掘る	セーターに穴があります
ぼけつをほる	セーターにあながあります

338.

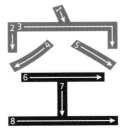

339.

Empty ~ Sky

In an empty cave
Pg.337

The construction keeps me dry
Pg.229

From the raining sky

On'yomi	*Kun'yomi*

On'yomi

クウ

Airport
空港
くうこう

Kun'yomi

そら

Clear sky・晴れた空・はれたそ

から

Karate・空手・からて
(Literally means empty hand
as you hold no weapons)

341.

Long ~ Leader

Top hat on her head

Long hair in a ponytail

She's the town's **leader**

On'yomi

Mayor
市長
しちょう

Kun'yomi

Long dog
長い犬
ながい いぬ

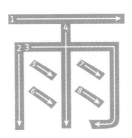

343.

Rain

Rain drips down my coat

Wind tugs at my umbrella

Hope the sun comes out

On'yomi

Rainy season
雨季
うき

Kun'yomi

Rainy day
雨の日
あめのひ

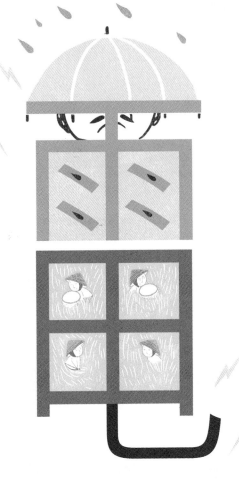

Electricity

Rain in a rice field
Pg.343 *Pg.21*

Through my umbrella handle
Pg.15

Electricity

On'yomi		*Kun'yomi*
テン		N/A

Train (electric)
電車
でんしゃ

You Did It!

やったー

You have now covered 162 Kanji!
We hope you have enjoyed this method and it has
helped introduce you to an incredible writing system.

There are hundreds more Kanji we would love to cover. If you'd
like to see more from us then please help support our project by
leaving a review, following us on Instagram, recommending us
to your friends and telling your sensei about Haiku.

We genuinely love seeing your pics and reading your messages.
Please do not hesitate to get in touch with any queries, nice
words or constructive feedback. We want to make the best
product we can and always try to implement your suggestions.

@hai_hiragana • hello@haihiragana.com

Thank You

Hai!Ku is a passion project of ours which we started just after moving to Japan in 2020. We had a lot of unexpected time indoors, which definitely helped in its creation! It was an interesting time and we couldn't have done it without help.

First and foremost, to our friends & family back in England and France who supported us and helped to keep Hai! Hiragana going while we were out of the country. With stacks of boxes around your houses and many packages popped in the post. Thank you!

To the native speakers, bilingual and teacher friends who helped test the method and double-check our spelling & grammar. Thank you!

Finally to the wonderful community of Japanese learners & enthusiasts. It is just the two of us making a project for learners by learners. We couldn't have done it without your support, feedback and kind words to motivate us. Thank you!

ありがとう
ございました!

How does a Japanese cat say thank you?
Ari-cat-ou

Bits & Bobs

We encourage using multiple methods while learning Japanese to better help it stick. We've included this handy chart so you can see how the radicals we used commonly appear.

Hai!Ku Name	Radical	Common Name
Samurai sword	丨	Line ~ Rod
Notebook	ノ	Slash ~ Bend
Beret	亠	Lid
Eight variant	ハ	Animal legs
Long Legs	儿	Human legs
Eight variant	丷	Grass ~ Horns
Cardboard box	冂	Upside down box
Umbrella handle	乚	Second ~ Latter
Seven	ヒ	Spoon
Truck (To)	卜	Divination
Moose	ム	Private
Two moose	幺	Short thread
Winter	夂	Follow
Leaves	艹	Grass ~ Vegetation
Go (half)	彳	Step
Measure	寸	Thumb ~ Sundial
Snowflakes	冫	Ice

Hiragana & Katakana

In case you're kana is rusty, you can download and print charts for free at www.haihiragana.com or scan the QR code below.

350.

Kanji Index

Hai!ku

Thank you for reading - It was really fun to make - We hope you liked it